SOME CORNER *of a* FOREIGN FIELD

SOME CORNER of a FOREIGN FIELD

POETRY of THE GREAT WAR

Edited by
JAMES BENTLEY

LITTLE, BROWN AND COMPANY
Boston   Toronto   London

Introduction, biographies and selection © 1992 by James Bentley
The moral right of the author has been asserted.

First published in Great Britain in 1992 by
Little, Brown and Company (UK) Limited
Brettenham House, Lancaster Place
London WC2E 7EN

Reprinted 1998

ISBN 0–316–88899–0

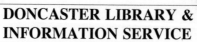

Title Page: A SHELL DUMP, FRANCE, *William P. Roberts*

CONTENTS

INTRODUCTION

> Here dead lie we because we did not choose
> To live and shame the land from which we sprung.
> Life, to be sure, is nothing much to lose,
> But young men think it is, and we were young.

So A.E. Housman lamented the men slaughtered in the Great War. His bitter sentiments are familiar, for he was but one of many poets who, whether or not they saw active service, felt compelled to write of a war in which eight million soldiers, airmen and seamen fought and died.

Often, the cataclysm heightened the perception of these poets to scenes, both at 'HOME AND ABROAD', which they might never see again. Edward Thomas writes of the ploughman, now lying dead on French soil, who used to sleep under the stars in his native Wiltshire. The Revd G.A. Studdert Kennedy, poet and padre (whom the troops called Woodbine Willie), evokes brothels in London and brothels abroad. Franics Ledwidge, an Irish poet, seems to hear a women weeping on the heights of Crocknaharna, twenty hundred miles away. On the flat slope of St Eloi, T.E. Hulme sees desultory men walking among dead horses and over a dead Belgian's belly, as casually as if they were tramping through Piccadilly.

To such heightened consciousnesses, even the devastation could be exhilarating. 'Then we were caught in a tornado of shells,' Owen wrote. 'The various "waves" were all broken up, and we carried on like a crowd moving off a cricket field.' He was describing not the end of a cricket match, but the experience of going over the top. 'When I looked back and saw the ground all crawling and wormy with wounded bodies, I felt no horror at all, but only an immense exhaltation at having got through the barrage.'

The sporting metaphor, by which playing fields were mentally transported to the hideous field of battle, was particularly potent. T.P. Cameron Wilson's 'Sportsmen in Paradise' ends:

<blockquote>
'God! but it's England,' someone said,
'And there's a cricket field!'
</blockquote>

Seeing his former pupils slaughtered one by one on foreign fields, the Eton housemaster and poet Hugh MacNaghten anxiously wrote to those still alive, relaying news of their old school. In one poignant note, he added that Andrew Thorne, a former student who had seen front-line action almost continuously for two years since August 1914, had written, 'We are going to play the field game on Friday, Germans permitting.'

For many, despite longing for their homeland, World War I began on a note of 'COURAGE AND CHIVALRY'. Some even relished a delicious frisson of danger. In 'Long Ages Past', written in October 1914, Wilfred Owen (who would later describe Horace's tag 'It is sweet and noble to die for one's country' as 'the old lie') exulted in the war as 'the last fulfilment of all the wicked, and of all the beautiful'. In his 'In Memoriam S.C.W., V.C.', Charles Hamilton Sorley describes the death of a schoolfellow killed in action on 30 July 1915 as, 'A glory that can never die'. Such proclamations were, in part, a means of defence against an intolerable reality. Many poets took the same line in contemplating their own possible sacrifice, most notably Rupert Brooke, whose poem 'The Soldier' gives the title to this book. As he set off for the Dardanelles, Brooke wrote, 'I've never been quite so happy in my life.' He added, 'I suddenly realize that the ambition of my life has been – since I was two – to go on a military expedition against Constantinople.'

Many war poets followed Brooke's example in comparing themselves to the heroes of ancient Greece, and war propagandists sought to play on the notion that the Great War was part of some worthy tradition. E.B. Osborn's anthology *The Muse in Arms*, which was published in 1917, boasts that, 'The Germans, and even our allies, cannot understand why this stout old nation persists in thinking of war as a sport; they do not know that sportsmanship is our new homely name, derived from a racial prediliction for comparing great things with small, for the *chevalerie* of the Middle Ages.' Courage was aligned with chivalry; the heroic past played out by gallant lads fighting in the present.

Some saw through this from the start. One was D.H. Lawrence, whose 'Rondeau of a Conscientious Objector' celebrates the courage of those brave enough to reject the prevailing jingoism. Yet the war drew into its spell others who had at first condemned it. On being asked for a war poem, W.B. Yeats wrote:

<blockquote>
I think it better that in times like these
A poet's mouth should be silent;
</blockquote>

but eventually composed the magnificent 'An Irish Airman Foresees His Death'. Similarly, Francis Ledwidge, already involved in the struggle for Irish freedom, forsook politics, elected to fight for England in its 'support of small nations', and thus met his doom.

As the war progressed, however, all the jingoism and the blithe sporting metaphors proved increasingly inadequate and the mood of many poets turned to 'Bitterness and Rage'. Reading Brooke's 'The Soldier' from the pulpit of his cathedral, the dean of St Paul's seemed to have sanctified the war. But in response to those who drew facile comparisons between the sacrifice of Jesus and the slaughter of young men, Wilfred Owen observed that Jesus never preached 'salvation by *death in war*'. In 'Gethsemane' (a poem of much subtlety, which T.S. Eliot himself claimed not fully to understand) Rudyard Kipling compares Jesus praying in the garden of Gethsemane to be spared crucifixion with the equally futile prayers of soldiers in the trenches.

Inevitably, many turned to curse God, who (in the words of the atheist A.E. Housman) had failed to bow out of heaven to see and save them. Prayer had become blasphemy, noted Wilfred Owen in 1918 as he composed 'Last Words'.

Kipling remained patriotic. After the war, his verses were carved on memorials to the dead, particularly the last stanza of his 'For All We Have and Are':

There is but one task for all –
One life for each to give.
What stands if Freedom fall?
Who dies if England live?

But in 1915, Kipling's only son had been killed in action and he had cried out in anguish:

My son was killed while laughing at some jest. I would I knew
What it was, and it might serve me in a time when jests are few.

Increasingly, in poems such as 'Destroyers in Collision' and 'Unknown Female Corpse', his vision of the Great War grew vicious.

At first such bitterness proved unwelcome to civilians back home. Early in 1916 the most bitter of all the war poets, Siegfried Sassoon, submitted what he called 'The first of my "outspoken" war poems' to the *Westminster Review*. It was rejected, as the publishers thought it might prejudice recruiting. More and more, however, men and women at home and abroad began to rail against the statesmen who had been responsible for the war. In 'The Parable of the Old Man and the Young', Owen compared them to Abram who, instead of sparing his son Isaac (as the Biblical story has it) refused to relent, even though an angel urged him to show mercy. The poem ends:

> But the old man would not do so, but slew his son,
> And half the seed of Europe, one by one.

G.K. Chesterton's 'Elegy in a Country Churchyard' laments that, unlike the flower of England's youth, these old men have no graves as yet. Siegfried Sassoon even hated official attempts to honour the dead with war memorials. Sir Reginald Blomfield's Menin Gate at Ypres was, to Sassoon, 'a pile of peace-complacent stone'.

> Well might the Dead who struggled in this slime
> Rise and deride this sepulchre of crime,

was his vicious comment.

Eventually, as the slaughter and horror grew worse, it became clear that the wounded, wormy, crawling bodies, even if they might be enemy soldiers, were also human beings. Poets began to see the need for 'COMPASSION AND RECONCILIATION'. Thomas Hardy managed to remain sensitive to the ties between Germany and his own part of England, expressing this in 'The Pity of It' and in 'England to Germany in 1914', which recalls the 'storied towers' of the Rhine. In 'Often When Warring' he remembers how a soldier will often comfort a defeated enemy, almost unconsciously.

As in Edward Thomas's 'This is No Case of Petty Right or Wrong', it seemed better to hate the Kaiser rather than the poor German soldier, sailor or airman. 'I wish I 'adn't done it,' confesses one of Woodbine Willie's soldiers (in 'What's the Good', a poem too long to be included in this collection):

> There's a young 'un like our Richard,
> And I bashed 'is 'ead in two,
> And there's that ole grey-'aired geezer
> Which I stuck 'is belly through.

In Sassoon's 'Glory of Women', the poet evokes not a British but a German mother, dreaming by the fire. While she is knitting socks to send to her son, his face is trodden deeper in the mud. And as Isaac Rosenberg, Studdert Kennedy, Charles Hamilton Sorley and Wilfred Owen asserted, death made comrades of former enemies.

An equally remarkable group of artists matched these war poets. Some shared the gentle, pastoral tradition in which the poets had also been nurtured. Others, such as John and Paul Nash, followed many poets across the line between serenity and bitterness. Eric Henri Kennington captured the youthful innocence of soldiers, and also their emotional torture in the trenches. Painters such as C.R.W. Nevinson and Wyndham Lewis were enthralled as well as repelled by the brutality of the Great War. Marine artists shared Kipling's relish for great ships. William Orpen's *Dead Germans in a Trench* reflects the compassion of the later war poems, while Colin Gill's *Heavy Artillery* has subtly mirrored those who perceived the war as blasphemy by introducing a crucifix, tumbled upside-down beside the guns.

And throughout all this, the women mourned, raged, forgave and dreamed. This anthology hears their voices too: Katharine Tynan, Alice Meynell. They kept the home fires burning, but many of their boys did not come home. Helen Thomas recalled the last time she saw her husband, as he set off through the mist to war. 'I heard his old call coming up to me: "Coo-ee!" he called. "Coo-ee!" I answered.' So they called, until there was no more sound. 'Panic seized me, and I ran through the mist and the snow to the top of the hill, and stood there a moment dumbly, with straining eyes and ears. There was nothing but the mist and the snow and the silence of death.'

JAMES BENTLEY, 1992

HOME and ABROAD

We'll walk no more on Cotswold
Where the sheep feed

IVOR GURNEY

THE UNDERWORLD: TAKING COVER IN A TUBE STATION
DURING A LONDON AIR RAID,
Walter Bayes.

GLOUCESTERSHIRE LANDSCAPE, *John Nash.*

SUMMER *in* ENGLAND, 1914

On London fell a clearer light;
    Caressing pencils of the sun
Defined the distances, the white
    Houses transfigured one by one,
The 'long, unlovely street' impearled.
O what a sky has walked the world!

Most happy year! And out of town
    The hay was prosperous, and the wheat;
The silken harvest climbed the down:
    Moon after moon was heavenly-sweet,
Stroking the bread within the sheaves,
Looking 'twixt apples and their leaves.

And while this rose made round her cup,
    The armies died convulsed. And when
This chaste young silver sun went up
    Softly, a thousand shattered men,
One wet corruption heaped the plain,
After a league-long throb of pain.

Flower following tender flower; and birds,
    And berries; and benignant skies
Made thrive the serried flocks and herds. –
    Yonder are men shot through the eyes.
        Love, hide thy face
From man's unpardonable race.

Who said 'No man hath greater love than this,
    To die to serve his friend'?
So these have loved us all unto the end.
    Chide thou no more, O thou unsacrificed!
The soldier dying dies upon a kiss,
    The very kiss of Christ.

ALICE MEYNELL

Magpies in Picardy

The magpies in Picardy
Are more than I can tell.
They flicker down the dusty roads
And cast a magic spell
On the men who march through Picardy,
Through Picardy to Hell.

(The blackbird flies with panic,
The swallow goes like light,
The finches move like ladies,
The owl floats by at night;
But the great and flashing magpie
He flies as artists might.)

A magpie in Picardy
Told me secret things –
Of the music in white feathers,
And the sunlight that sings
And dances in deep shadows –
He told me with his wings.

(The hawk is cruel and rigid,
He watches from a height;
The rook is slow and sombre,
The robin loves to fight;
But the great and flashing magpie
He flies as lovers might.)

He told me that in Picardy,
An age ago or more,
While all his fathers still were eggs,
These dusty highways bore
Brown singing soldiers marching out
Through Picardy to war.

T.P. Cameron Wilson

THE BALLOON APRON, *Frank Dobson.*

Sportsmen in Paradise

They left the fury of the fight,
And they were very tired.
The gates of Heaven were open, quite
Unguarded, and unwired.
There was no sound of any gun;
The land was still and green:
Wide hills lay silent in the sun,
Blue valleys slept between.

They saw far off a little wood
Stand up against the sky.
Knee-deep in grass a great tree stood . . .
Some lazy cows went by . . .
There were some rooks sailed overhead –
And once a church-bell pealed.
'God! but it's England,' someone said,
'And there's a cricket field!'

T.P. Cameron Wilson

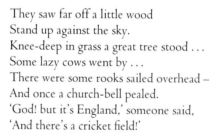

RUINED COUNTRY, *Paul Nash.*

OPPY WOOD, 1917, *John Nash.*

No One Cares Less Than I

'No one cares less than I,
Nobody knows but God,
Whether I am destined to lie
Under a foreign clod,'
Were the words I made to the bugle call in the morning.

But laughing, storming, scorning,
Only the bugles know
What the bugles say in the morning,
And they do not care, when they blow
The call that I heard and made words to early this
    morning.

EDWARD THOMAS

READY TO START (SELF-PORTRAIT), *William Orpen.*

TO HIS LOVE

He's gone, and all our plans
  Are useless indeed.
We'll walk no more on Cotswold
  Where the sheep feed
  Quietly and take no heed.

His body that was so quick
  Is not as you
Knew it, on Severn river
  Under the blue
  Driving our small boat through.

You would not know him now . . .
  But still he died
Nobly, so cover him over
  With violets of pride
  Purple from Severn side.

Cover him, cover him soon!
  And with thick-set
Masses of memoried flowers –
  Hide that red wet
  Thing I must somehow forget.

IVOR GURNEY

A Girl's Song

The Meuse and Marne have little waves;
  The slender poplars o'er them lean.
One day they will forget the graves
  That give the grass its living green.

Some brown French girl the rose will wear
  That springs above his comely head;
Will twine it in her russet hair,
  Nor wonder why it is so red.

His blood is in the rose's veins,
  His hair is in the yellow corn.
My grief is in the weeping rains
  And in the keening wind forlorn.

Flow softly, softly, Marne and Meuse;
  Tread lightly all ye browsing sheep;
Fall tenderly, O silver dews,
  For here my dear Love lies asleep.

The earth is on his sealèd eyes,
  The beauty marred that was my pride;
Would I were lying where he lies,
  And sleeping sweetly by his side!

The Spring will come by Meuse and Marne,
  The birds be blithesome in the tree.
I heap the stones to make his cairn
  Where many sleep as sound as he.

KATHARINE TYNAN

TEA IN THE BED-SITTER, *Harold Gilman.*

A TORPEDOED TRAMP STEAMER OFF THE LONGSHIPS, CORNWALL, *Geoffrey S. Allfree.*

CROCKNAHARNA

On the heights of Crocknaharna,
(Oh, the lure of Crocknaharna)
On a morning fair and early
Of a dear remembered May,
There I heard a colleen singing
In the brown rocks and the grey.
She, the pearl of Crocknaharna,
Crocknaharna, Crocknaharna,
Wild with gulls is Crocknaharna
Twenty hundred miles away.

On the heights of Crocknaharna,
(Oh, thy sorrow Crocknaharna)
On an evening dim and misty
Of a cold November day,
There I heard a woman weeping
In the brown rocks and the grey.
Oh, the pearl of Crocknaharna
(Crocknaharna, Crocknaharna),
Black with grief is Crocknaharna
Twenty hundred miles away.

FRANCIS LEDWIDGE

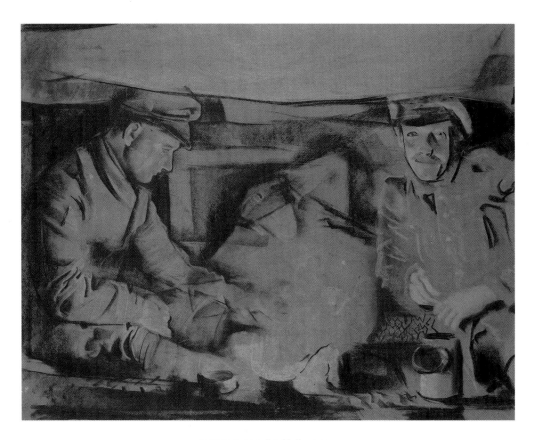

THE DIE-HARDS, *Eric H. Kennington.*

WILLIAM GLADSTONE, M.C.

(COLDSTREAM GUARDS.)

Killed in Action September 27, 1918.
CAPTAIN OF HIS TUTOR'S, 1916.

Brave oarsman, of the gracious silence, loved
    By all, my captain, once I did you wrong,
Doubting your leading. Smilingly you proved
    Most gentle is most strong.

You came to us from France, and overwise
    I knew the brand of war must leave a trace;
But childhood's innocence was in your eyes,
    God's peace was on your face.

And you, and all the best are dead, and this
    Abides a riddle baffling human wit,
And Shakespeare has no word beyond 'It is;
    And my heart breaks at it.'

Yet this a child may know, The Shadow hides
    Life in the Presence, or the dreamless bed:
And still for all who mourn Love's word abides,
    'They shall be comforted.'

HUGH MACNAGHTEN

THE PLACE

Blossoms as old as May I scatter here,
And a blue wave I lifted from the stream.
It shall not know when winter days are drear
Or March is hoarse with blowing. But a-dream
The laurel boughs shall hold a canopy
Peacefully over it the winter long,
Till all the birds are back from oversea,
And April rainbows win a blackbird's song.

And when the war is over I shall take
My lute a-down to it and sing again
Songs of the whispering things amongst the brake,
And those I love shall know them by their strain.
Their airs shall be the blackbird's twilight song,
Their words shall be all flowers with fresh dews hoar –
But it is lonely now in winter long,
And, God! to hear the blackbird sing once more.

FRANCIS LEDWIDGE

GIRL IN BLUE, *Gwen John.*

TRENCHES: *ST ELOI*

Over the flat slope of St Eloi
A wide wall of sand bags.
Night,
In the silence desultory men
Pottering over small fires, cleaning their mess-tins:
To and fro, from the lines,
Men walk as on Piccadilly,
Making paths in the dark,
Through scattered dead horses,
Over a dead Belgian's belly.

The Germans have rockets. The English have no rockets.
Behind the line, cannon, hidden, lying back miles.
Before the line, chaos:

My mind is a corridor. The minds about me are corridors.
Nothing suggests itself. There is nothing to do but keep on.

T.E. HULME

SAPPERS AT WORK: A CANADIAN TUNNELLING COMPANY, *David Bomberg.*

First Time In

After the dread tales and red yarns of the Line
Anything might have come to us; but the divine
Afterglow brought us up to a Welsh colony
Hiding in sandbag ditches, whispering consolatory
Soft foreign things. Then we were taken in
To low huts candle-lit, shaded close by slitten
Oilsheets, and there the boys gave us kind welcome,
So that we looked out as from the edge of home.
Sang us Welsh things, and changed all former notions
To human hopeful things. And the next day's guns
Nor any line-pangs ever quite could blot out
That strangely beautiful entry to war's rout;
Candles they gave us, precious and shared over-rations –
Ulysses found little more in his wanderings without doubt.
'David of the White Rock', the 'Slumber Song' so soft, and that
Beautiful tune to which roguish words by Welsh pit boys
Are sung – but never more beautiful than there
                    under the guns' noise.

Ivor Gurney

FARM AT WATENDLATH, *Dora Carrington*.

OBSERVATION OF FIRE, *Colin U. Gill.*

A Private

This ploughman dead in battle slept out of doors
Many a frozen night, and merrily
Answered staid drinkers, good bedmen, and all bores:
'At Mrs. Greenland's Hawthorn Bush,' said he,
'I slept.' None knew which bush. Above the town,
Beyond 'The Drover,' a hundred spot the down
In Wiltshire. And where now at last he sleeps
More sound in France – that, too, he secret keeps.

EDWARD THOMAS

COURAGE
and CHIVALRY

Now, God be thanked
Who has matched us with His hour.

RUPERT BROOKE

AN IMPRESSION OF LENS, FRANCE, SEEN FROM AN AEROPLANE,
Richard C. Carline.

THE KENSINGTONS AT LAVENTIE, *Eric H. Kennington*.

THE SOLDIER

If I should die, think only this of me:
    That there's some corner of a foreign field
That is for ever England. There shall be
    In that rich earth a richer dust concealed;
A dust whom England bore, shaped, made aware,
    Gave, once, her flowers to love, her ways to
       roam,
A body of England's, breathing English air,
    Washed by the rivers, blest by suns of home.
And think, this heart, all evil shed away,
    A pulse in the eternal mind, no less
      Gives somewhere back the thoughts by
        England given;
Her sights and sounds; dreams happy as her day;
    And laughter, learnt of friends; and gentleness,
      In hearts at peace, under an English heaven.

RUPERT BROOKE

An Irish Airman Foresees His Death

I know that I shall meet my fate
Somewhere among the clouds above;
Those that I fight I do not hate,
Those that I guard I do not love;
My country is Kiltartan Cross,
My countrymen Kiltartan's poor,
No likely end could bring them loss
Or leave them happier than before.
Nor law, nor duty bade me fight,
Nor public men, nor cheering crowds.

A lonely impulse of delight
Drove to this tumult in the clouds;
I balanced all, brought all to mind,
The years to come seemed waste of breath,
A waste of breath the years behind
In balance with this life, this death.

W. B. YEATS

BRITISH SCOUTS LEAVING THEIR AERODROME ON PATROL, OVER THE ASIAGO PLATEAU, ITALY,
Sydney W. Carline.

LA MITRAILLEUSE, *C.R.W. Nevinson.*

Long Ages Past

Long ages past in Egypt thou wert worshipped
And thou wert wrought from ivory and beryl.
They brought thee jewels and they brought
   their slain,
Thy feet were dark with blood of sacrifice.
From dawn to midnight, O my painted idol,
Thou satest smiling, and the noise of killing
Was harp and timbrel in thy pale jade ears;
The livid dead were given thee for toys.

Thou wert a mad slave in a Persian palace,
And the King loved thee for thy furious beauty,
And all men heard thy ravings with a smile
Because thy face was fairer than a flower.
But with a little knife so wantonly
Thou slewest women and thy pining lovers,
And on thy lips the stain of crimson blood,
And on thy brow the pallor of their death.

Thou art the dream beheld by frenzied princes
In smoke of opium. Thou art the last fulfilment
Of all the wicked, and of all the beautiful.
We hold thee as a poppy to our mouths,
Finding with thee forgetfulness of God.
Thou art the face reflected in a mirror
Of wild desire, of pain, of bitter pleasure.
The witches shout thy name beneath the moon,
The fires of Hell have held thee in their fangs.

WILFRED OWEN

Mine Sweepers

1914–18
(*Sea Warfare*)

Dawn off the Foreland – the young flood making
    Jumbled and short and steep –
Black in the hollows and bright where it's breaking –
    Awkward water to sweep.
    'Mines reported in the fairway,
    'Warn all traffic and detain.
''Sent up *Unity*, *Claribel*, *Assyrian*, *Stormcock*, and *Golden Gain*.'

Noon off the Foreland – the first ebb making
    Lumpy and strong in the bight.
Boom after boom, and the golf-hut shaking
    And the jackdaws wild with fright!
    'Mines located in the fairway,
    'Boats now working up the chain,
'Sweepers – *Unity*, *Claribel*, *Assyrian*, *Stormcock*, and *Golden Gain*.'

Dusk off the Foreland – the last light going
    And the traffic crowding through,
And five damned trawlers with their syreens blowing
    Heading the whole review!
    'Sweep completed in the fairway.
    'No more mines remain.
''Sent back *Unity*, *Claribel*, *Assyrian*, *Stormcock*, and *Golden Gain*.'

RUDYARD KIPLING

DAZZLE-SHIPS IN DRYDOCK AT LIVERPOOL, *Edward Wadsworth.*

IN BILLETS, WINTER: RATIONS UP, *Herbert A. Budd.*

PEACE

Now, God be thanked Who has matched us with His hour,
    And caught our youth, and wakened us from sleeping,
With hand made sure, clear eye, and sharpened power,
    To turn, as swimmers into cleanness leaping,
Glad from a world grown old and cold and weary,
    Leave the sick hearts that honour could not move,
And half-men, and their dirty songs and dreary,
    And all the little emptiness of love!

Oh! we, who have known shame, we have found release there,
    Where there's no ill, no grief, but sleep has mending.
        Naught broken save this body, lost but breath;
Nothing to shake the laughing heart's long peace there
    But only agony, and that has ending;
        And the worst friend and enemy is but Death.

RUPERT BROOKE

49

MEN WHO MARCH AWAY

(Song of the Soldiers)

What of the faith and fire within us
    Men who march away
    Ere the barn-cocks say
    Night is growing gray,
Leaving all that here can win us;
What of the faith and fire within us
    Men who march away?

Is it a purblind prank, O think you,
    Friend with the musing eye,
    Who watch us stepping by
    With doubt and dolorous sigh?
Can much pondering so hoodwink you!
Is it a purblind prank, O think you,
    Friend with the musing eye?

Nay. We well see what we are doing,
    Though some may not see –
    Dalliers as they be –
    England's need are we;
Her distress would leave us rueing:
Nay. We well see what we are doing,
    Though some may not see!

In our heart of hearts believing
    Victory crowns the just,
    And that braggarts must
    Surely bite the dust,
Press we to the field ungrieving,
In our heart of hearts believing
    Victory crowns the just.

Hence the faith and fire within us
    Men who march away
    Ere the barn-cocks say
    Night is growing gray,
Leaving all that here can win us;
Hence the faith and fire within us
    Men who march away.

THOMAS HARDY

ON THE DEPARTURE PLATFORM, *Bernard Meninsky*.

THE SOMME BATTLEFIELD, *Miss Oliver.*

IN FLANDERS FIELDS

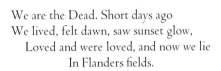

In Flanders fields the poppies blow
Between the crosses, row on row,
    That mark our place; and in the sky
    The larks, still bravely singing, fly
Scarce heard amid the guns below.

We are the Dead. Short days ago
We lived, felt dawn, saw sunset glow,
    Loved and were loved, and now we lie
        In Flanders fields.

Take up our quarrel with the foe:
To you from failing hands we throw
    The torch; be yours to hold it high.
    If ye break faith with us who die
We shall not sleep, though poppies grow
        In Flanders fields.

JOHN McCRAE

RENDEZVOUS

I have a rendezvous with Death
At some disputed barricade,
When spring comes back with rustling shade
And apple-blossoms fill the air –
I have a rendezvous with Death
When spring brings back blue days and fair.

It may be he shall take my hand
And lead me into his dark land
And close my eyes and quench my breath –
It may be I shall pass him still.
I have a rendezvous with Death
On some scarred slope of battered hill,
When Spring comes round again this year
And the first meadow-flowers appear.

God knows 'twere better to be deep
Pillowed in silk and scented down,
Where love throbs out in blissful sleep,
Pulse nigh to pulse, and breath to breath,
Where hushed awakenings are dear . . .
But I've a rendezvous with Death
At midnight in some flaming town,
When spring trips north again this year,
And I to my pledge word am true,
I shall not fail that rendezvous.

ALAN SEEGER

EVENING, AFTER A PUSH, *Colin U. Gill.*

BOMBARDMENT

The Town has opened to the sun.
Like a flat red lily with a million petals
She unfolds, she comes undone.

A sharp sky brushes upon
The myriad glittering chimney-tips
As she gently exhales to the sun.

Hurrying creatures run
Down the labyrinth of the sinister flower.
What is it they shun?

A dark bird falls from the sun.
It curves in a rush to the heart of the vast
Flower: the day has begun.

D.H. LAWRENCE

THE BOMBARDMENT OF GORIZIA, 21 AUGUST 1917, *Elliott Seabrooke.*

WE ARE MAKING A NEW WORLD, *Paul Nash.*

RONDEAU *of the* CONSCIENTIOUS OBJECTOR

The hours have tumbled their leaden, monotonous sands
And piled them up in a dull grey heap in the west.
I carry my patience sullenly through the waste lands;
To-morrow will pour them all back, the dull hours I detest.

I force my cart through the sodden filth that is pressed
Into ooze, and the sombre dirt spouts up at my hands
As I make my way in twilight now to rest.
The hours have tumbled their leaden, monotonous sands.

A twisted thorn-tree still in the evening stands
Defending the memory of leaves and the happy round nest.
But mud has flooded the homes of these weary lands
And piled them up in a dull grey heap in the west.

All day has the clank of iron on iron distressed
The nerve-bare place. Now a little silence expands
And a gasp of relief. But the soul is still compressed;
I carry my patience sullenly through the waste lands.

The hours have ceased to fall, and a star commands
Shadows to cover our stricken manhood, and blest
Sleep to make us forget: but he understands:
To-morrow will pour them all back, the dull hours I detest.

D.H. LAWRENCE

THE LANDSCAPE, HILL 60, *Paul Nash.*

The Silent One

Who died on the wires, and hung there, one of two –
Who for his hours of life had chattered through
Infinite lovely chatter of Bucks accent:
Yet faced unbroken wires; stepped over, and went
A noble fool, faithful to his stripes – and ended.
But I weak, hungry, and willing only for the chance
Of line – to fight in the line, lay down under unbroken
Wires, and saw the flashes and kept unshaken,
Till the politest voice – a finicking accent, said:
'Do you think you might crawl through there: there's a hole.'
Darkness, shot at: I smiled, as politely replied –
'I'm afraid not, Sir.' There was no hole no way to be seen,
Nothing but chance of death, after tearing of clothes.
Kept flat, and watched the darkness, hearing bullets whizzing –
And thought of music – and swore deep heart's deep oaths
(Polite to God) and retreated and came on again,
Again retreated – and a second time faced the screen.

Ivor Gurney

IN MEMORIAM S.C.W., V.C.

There is no fitter end than this.
    No need is now to yearn nor sigh.
We know the glory that is his,
    A glory that can never die.

Surely we knew it long before,
    Knew all along that he was made
For a swift radiant morning, for
    A sacrificing swift night-shade.

CHARLES HAMILTON SORLEY

OVER THE TOP, *John Nash.*

BITTERNESS
and RAGE

The War was not strife
it was murder

D.H. LAWRENCE

TROOPS RESTING (detail), *C.R.W. Nevinson.*

YOUTH MOURNING, *George Clausen.*

JOINING *the* COLOURS

(West Kents, Dublin, August 1914)

There they go marching all in step so gay!
  Smooth-cheeked and golden, food for shells and guns.
Blithely they go as to a wedding day,
      The mothers' sons.

The drab street stares to see them row on row
  On the high tram-tops, singing like the lark.
Too careless-gay for courage, singing they go
      Into the dark.

With tin whistles, mouth-organs, any noise,
  They pipe the way to glory and the grave;
Foolish and young, the gay and golden boys
      Love cannot save.

High heart! High courage! The poor girls they kissed
  Run with them: they shall kiss no more, alas!
Out of the mist they stepped – into the mist
      Singing they pass.

KATHARINE TYNAN

*L*AST *W*ORDS

'O Jesus Christ!' one fellow sighed.
And kneeled, and bowed, tho' not in prayer, and died.
    And the Bullets sang 'In Vain',
    Machine Guns chuckled 'Vain',
    Big Guns guffawed 'In Vain'.

'Father and mother!' one boy said.
Then smiled – at nothing, like a small child; being dead.
    And the Shrapnel Cloud
    Slowly gestured 'Vain',
    The falling splinters muttered 'Vain'.

'My love!' another cried, 'My love, my bud!'
Then, gently lowered, his whole face kissed the mud.
    And the Flares gesticulated, 'Vain',
    The Shells hooted, 'In Vain',
    And the Gas hissed, 'In Vain'.

WILFRED OWEN

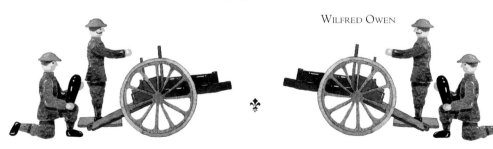

OPERATING ON A SLIGHTLY WOUNDED MAN IN A REGIMENTAL AID POST, *Austin O. Spare.*

BOMBING: NIGHT, *William Orpen.*

My Peace
I Leave With You

Thy Peace! Thou pale, despisèd Christ!
  What Peace is there in Thee,
Nailed to the Cross that crowns the world,
      In agony?

No Peace of home was Thine; no rest
  When Thy day's work was done.
When darkness called the world to sleep
      And veiled the sun,

No children gathered round Thy knee,
  No hand soothed care away:
Thou hadst not where to lay Thy head
      At close of day.

What Peace was Thine? Misunderstood,
  Rejected by Thine own,
Pacing Thy grim Gethsemane,
      Outcast and lone.

What Peace hast Thou to give the world?
  There is enough of pain;
Always upon my window beats
      The sound of rain.

The source of sorrow is not dried,
  Nor stays the stream of tears,
But winds on weeping to the sea,
      All down the years.

For millions come to Golgotha
  To suffer and to die,
Forsaken in their hour of need,
      And asking, Why?

Man's Via Crucis never ends,
  Earth's Calvaries increase,
The world is full of spears and nails,
      But where is Peace?

'Take up Thy Cross and follow Me,
  I am the Way, my son,
Via Crucis, Via Pacis,
      Meet and are one.'

G.A. Studdert Kennedy

THE GENERAL

'Good-morning; good-morning!' the General said
When we met him last week on our way to the line.
Now the soldiers he smiled at are most of 'em dead,
And we're cursing his staff for incompetent swine.
'He's a cheery old card,' grunted Harry to Jack
As they slogged up to Arras with rifle and pack.

But he did for them both by his plan of attack.

SIEGFRIED SASSOON

A GROUP OF SOLDIERS, *C.R.W. Nevinson.*

ELEGY *in a*
COUNTRY CHURCHYARD

The men that worked for England
They have their graves at home:
And bees and birds of England
About the cross can roam.

But they that fought for England,
Following a falling star,
Alas, alas for England
They have their graves afar.

And they that rule in England,
In stately conclave met,
Alas, alas for England
They have no graves as yet.

G.K. CHESTERTON

A GROUP OF SOLDIERS, *C.R.W. Nevinson.*

ELEGY *in a* COUNTRY CHURCHYARD

The men that worked for England
They have their graves at home:
And bees and birds of England
About the cross can roam.

But they that fought for England,
Following a falling star,
Alas, alas for England
They have their graves afar.

And they that rule in England,
In stately conclave met,
Alas, alas for England
They have no graves as yet.

G.K. Chesterton

SUNSET: RUIN OF THE HOSPICE, WYTSCHAETE, *Paul Nash.*

WOUNDED MEN ON DUPPAS HILL, CROYDON, *Dorothy J. Coke.*

GETHSEMANE 1914-18

The Garden called Gethsemane
  In Picardy it was,
And there the people came to see
  The English soldiers pass.
We used to pass – we used to pass
  Or halt, as it might be.

And ship our masks in case of gas
  Beyond Gethsemane.

The Garden called Gethsemane,
  It held a pretty lass,
But all the time she talked to me
  I prayed my cup might pass.
The officer sat on the chair,
  The men lay on the grass,
And all the time we halted there
  I prayed my cup might pass.

It didn't pass – it didn't pass –
  It didn't pass from me.
I drank it when we met the gas
  Beyond Gethsemane!

RUDYARD KIPLING

THE LATE WAR

The War was not strife
it was murder
each side trying to murder the other side
evilly.

MURDER

Killing is not evil.
A man may be my enemy to the death,
and that is passion and communion.

But murder is always evil
being an act of one
perpetrated upon the other
without cognisance or communion.

MURDEROUS WEAPONS

So guns and strong explosives
are evil, evil
they let death upon unseen men
in sheer murder.

And most murderous of all devices
are poison gases and air-bombs
refinements of evil.

D.H. LAWRENCE

THE BATTLE OF 'THE PIPS', 24 APRIL 1917, *William T. Wood.*

❖

GREATER LOVE

Red lips are not so red
    As the stained stones kissed by the English dead.
Kindness of wooed and wooer
Seems shame to their love pure.
O Love, your eyes lose lure
    When I behold eyes blinded in my stead!

Your slender attitude
    Trembles not exquisite like limbs knife-skewed,
Rolling and rolling there
Where God seems not to care;
Till the fierce love they bear
    Cramps them in death's extreme decrepitude.

Your voice sings not so soft, –
    Though even as wind murmuring through raftered loft, –
Your dear voice is not dear,
Gentle, and evening clear,
As theirs whom none now hear,
    Now earth has stopped their piteous mouths that coughed.

Heart, you were never hot
    Nor large, nor full like hearts made great with shot;
And though your hand be pale,
Paler are all which trail
Your cross through flame and hail:
    Weep, you may weep, for you may touch them not.

WILFRED OWEN

ADVANCED DRESSING STATION ON THE STRUMA, *Henry Lamb.*

THE WOMEN'S LAND ARMY AND GERMAN PRISONERS, *Randolphe Schwabe.*

DESTROYERS in COLLISION

For Fog and Fate no charm is found
  To lighten or amend.
I, hurrying to my bride, was drowned –
  Cut down by my best friend.

UNKNOWN FEMALE CORPSE

Headless, lacking foot and hand,
Horrible I come to land.
I beseech all women's sons
Know I was a mother once.

CONVOY ESCORT

I was a shepherd to fools
  Causelessly bold or afraid.
They would not abide by my rules.
  Yet they escaped. For I stayed.

RAPED and REVENGED

One used and butchered me: another spied
Me broken – for which thing an hundred died.
So it was learned among the heathen hosts
How much a freeborn woman's favour costs.

 RUDYARD KIPLING

'BLIGHTERS'

The House is crammed: tier beyond tier they grin
And cackle at the Show, while prancing ranks
Of harlots shrill the chorus, drunk with din;
'We're sure the Kaiser loves our dear old Tanks!'

I'd like to see a Tank come down the stalls,
Lurching to ragtime tunes, or 'Home, sweet Home',
And there'd be no more jokes in Music-halls
To mock the riddled corpses round Bapaume.

SIEGFRIED SASSOON

THE ADVANCE, *W. Bernard Adeney.*

INTERROGATION, *Francis Dodd.*

THE ADVANCE, *W. Bernard Adeney.*

INTERROGATION, *Francis Dodd.*

INSPECTION

'You! What d'you mean by this?' I rapped.
'You dare come on parade like this?'
'Please, sir, it's – ' 'Old yer mouth,' the sergeant snapped.
'I takes 'is name, sir?' – 'Please, and then dismiss.'

Some days 'confined to camp' he got,
For being 'dirty on parade'.
He told me, afterwards, the damnèd spot
Was blood, his own. 'Well, blood is dirt,' I said.

'Blood's dirt,' he laughed, looking away,
Far off to where his wound had bled
And almost merged for ever into clay.
'The world is washing out its stains,' he said.
'It doesn't like our cheeks so red:
Young blood's its great objection.
But when we're duly white-washed, being dead,
The race will bear Field Marshal God's inspection.'

WILFRED OWEN

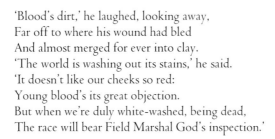

Compassion and Reconciliation

I am the enemy you killed,
my friend.

WILFRED OWEN

A BATTERY SHELLED,
Percy Wyndham Lewis.

DEAD GERMANS IN A TRENCH, *William Orpen.*

RECONCILIATION

When you are standing at your hero's grave,
or near some homeless village where he died,
Remember, through your heart's rekindling pride,
The German soldiers who were loyal and brave.

Men fought like brutes; and hideous things were done;
And you have nourished hatred, harsh and blind.
But in that Golgotha perhaps you'll find
The mothers of the men who killed your son.

SIEGFRIED SASSOON

This is No Case of Petty Right or Wrong

This is no case of petty right or wrong
That politicians or philosophers
Can judge. I hate not Germans, nor grow hot
With love of Englishmen, to please newspapers.
Beside my hate for one fat patriot
My hatred of the Kaiser is love true:-
A kind of god he is, banging a gong.
But I have not to choose between the two,
Or between justice and injustice. Dinned
With war and argument I read no more
Than in the storm smoking along the wind
Athwart the wood. Two witches' cauldrons roar.
From one the weather shall rise clear and gay;
Out of the other an England beautiful
And like her mother that died yesterday.
Little I know or care if, being dull,
I shall miss something that historians
Can rake out of the ashes when perchance
The phoenix broods serene above their ken.
But with the best and meanest Englishmen
I am one in crying, God save England, lest
We lose what never slaves and cattle blessed.
The ages made her that made us from dust:
She is all we know and live by, and we trust
She is good and must endure, loving her so:
And as we love ourselves we hate her foe.

EDWARD THOMAS

L'ENFER, *Georges Leroux.*

⚜

POILU AND TOMMY, *William Orpen.*

Often When Warring

Often when warring for he wist not what,
An enemy-soldier, passing by one weak,
Has tendered water, wiped the burning cheek,
And cooled the lips so black and clammed and hot;

Then gone his way, and maybe quite forgot
The deed of grace amid the roar and reek;
Yet larger vision than loud arms bespeak
He there has reached, although he has known it not

For natural mindsight, triumphing in the act
Over the throes of artificial rage,
Has thuswise muffled victory's peal of pride,
Rended to ribands policy's specious page
That deals but with evasion, code, and pact,
And war's apology wholly stultified.

Thomas Hardy

GLORY *of* WOMEN

You love us when we're heroes, home on leave,
Or wounded in a mentionable place.
You worship decorations; you believe
That chivalry redeems the war's disgrace.
You make us shells. You listen with delight,
By tales of dirt and danger fondly thrilled.
You crown our distant ardours while we fight,
And mourn our laurelled memories when we're killed.
You can't believe that British troops 'retire'
When hell's last horror breaks them, and they run,
Trampling the terrible corpses – blind with blood.
   O German mother dreaming by the fire,
     While you are knitting socks to send your son
     His face is trodden deeper in the mud.

SIEGFRIED SASSOON

THE SISTERS, *Edmund Dulac.*

SPRING IN THE TRENCHES, RIDGE WOOD, 1917, *Paul Nash.*

Break of Day in the Trenches

The darkness crumbles away.
It is the same old druid Time as ever,
Only a live thing leaps my hand,
A queer sardonic rat,
As I pull the parapet's poppy
To stick behind my ear.
Droll rat, they would shoot you if they knew
Your cosmopolitan sympathies.
Now you have touched this English hand
You will do the same to a German
Soon, no doubt, if it be your pleasure
To cross the sleeping green between.
It seems you inwardly grin as you pass

Strong eyes, fine limbs, haughty athletes,
Less chanced than you for life,
Bonds to the whims of murder,
Sprawled in the bowels of the earth,
The torn fields of France.
What do you see in our eyes
At the shrieking iron and flame
Hurled through still heavens?
What quaver – what heart aghast?
Poppies whose roots are in man's veins
Drop, and are ever dropping;
But mine in my ear is safe –
Just a little white with the dust.

Isaac Rosenberg

Sonnet

Such, such is Death: no triumph: no defeat:
Only an empty pail, a slate rubbed clean,
A merciful putting away of what has been.

And this we know: Death is not Life effete,
Life crushed, the broken pail. We who have seen
So marvellous things know well the end not yet.

Victor and vanquished are a-one in death:
Coward and brave: friend, foe. Ghosts do not say
'Come, what was your record when you drew breath?'
But a big blot has hid each yesterday
So poor, so manifestly incomplete.
And your bright Promise, withered long and sped,
Is touched, stirs, rises, opens and grows sweet
And blossoms and is you, when you are dead.

CHARLES HAMILTON SORLEY

THE SISTERS, *Edmund Dulac.*

SPRING IN THE TRENCHES, RIDGE WOOD, 1917, *Paul Nash.*

IRISH TROOPS IN THE JUDEAN HILLS SURPRISED BY A TURKISH BOMBARDMENT, *Henry Lamb.*

THE PITY of IT

I walked in loamy Wessex lanes, afar
From rail-track and from highway, and I heard
In field and farmstead many an ancient word
Of local lineage like 'Thu bist', 'Er war',

'Ich woll', 'Er sholl', and by-talk similar,
Nigh as they speak who in this month's moon grid
At England's very loins, thereunto spurred
By gangs whose glory threats and slaughters are.

Then seemed a Heart crying: 'Whosoever they be
At root and bottom of this, who flung this flame
Between kin folk kin tongued even as are we,

'Sinister, ugly, lurid, be their fame;
May their familiars grow to shun their name,
And their brood perish everlastingly.'

THOMAS HARDY

THE CAPTIVE, *Colin U. Gill.*

ARTILLERY DRIVERS IN THE SNOW, *A. Neville Lewis.*

At a Calvary Near the Ancre

One ever hangs where shelled roads part.
   In this war He too lost a limb,
But His disciples hide apart;
   And now the Soldiers bear with Him.

Near Golgotha strolls many a priest,
   And in their faces there is pride
That they were flesh-marked by the Beast
   By whom the gentle Christ's denied.

The scribes on all the people shove
   And brawl allegiance to the state,
But they who love the greater love
   Lay down their life; they do not hate.

WILFRED OWEN

'When You See Millions of the Mouthless Dead'

When you see millions of the mouthless dead
Across your dreams in pale battalions go,
Say not soft things as other men have said,
That you'll remember. For you need not so.
Give them not praise. For, deaf, how should they know
It is not curses heaped on each gashed head?
Nor tears. Their blind eyes see not your tears flow.
Nor honour. It is easy to be dead.
Say only this, 'They are dead.' Then add thereto,
'Yet many a better one has died before.'
Then, scanning all the o'ercrowded mass, should you
Perceive one face that you loved heretofore,
It is a spook. None wears the face you knew.
Great death has made all his for evermore.

CHARLES HAMILTON SORLEY

TRAVOYS ARRIVING WITH WOUNDED AT A DRESSING STATION AT SMOL, MACEDONIA,
SEPTEMBER 1916, *Stanley Spencer.*

A Gal of the Streets

'Verily I say unto you, the … harlots go into the
Kingdom of Heaven before you.'

I met 'er one night down in Leicester Square,
With paint on 'er lips and dye on 'er 'air,
With 'er fixed glad eye and 'er brazen stare, –
　　　She were a gal on the streets.

I was done with leave – on my way to France,
To the ball of death and the devil's dance;
I was raving mad – and glad of the chance
　　　To meet a gal on the streets.

I went with 'er 'ome – to the cursèd game,
And we talked of men with the talk of shame;
I 'appened to mention a dead pal's name,
　　　She were a gal on the streets.

'Your pal! Do you know 'im?' she stopped and
　　said:
' 'Ow is 'e? Where is 'e? I once knowed Ted.'
I stuttered and stamered aht – ' 'E's gorn-dead.'
　　　She were a gal on the streets.

She stood there and swayed like a drunken man,
And 'er face went green where 'er paint began,
Then she muttered, 'My Gawd, I carn't'; and
　　ran –
　　　She were a gal on the streets.

G.A. Studdert Kennedy

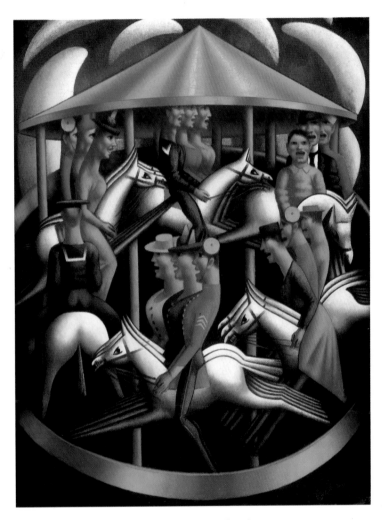

MERRY-GO-ROUND, *Mark Gertler.*

GASSED (detail), *John Singer Sargent.*

TO GERMANY

You are blind like us. Your hurt no man designed,
And no man claimed the conquest of your land.
But gropers both through fields of thought confined
We stumble and we do not understand.
You only saw your future bigly planned,
And we, the tapering paths of our own mind,
And in each other's dearest ways we stand,
And hiss and hate. And the blind fight the blind.

When it is peace, then we may view again
With new-won eyes each other's truer form
And wonder. Grown more loving-kind and warm
We'll grasp firm hands and laugh at the old pain,
When it is peace. But until peace, the storm
The darkness and the thunder and the rain.

CHARLES HAMILTON SORLEY

ENGLAND *to* GERMANY *in* 1914

'O England, may God punish thee!'
– Is it that Teuton genius flowers
Only to breathe malignity
Upon its friend of earlier hours?
– We have eaten your bread, you have eaten ours,
We have loved your burgs, your pines' green moan,
Fair Rhine-stream, and its storied towers;
Your shining souls of deathless dowers
Have won us as they were our own:

We have nursed no dreams to shed your blood,
We have matched your might not rancorously
Save a flushed few whose blatant mood
You heard and marked as well as we
To tongue not in their country's key;
But yet you cry with face aflame,
'O England, may God punish thee!'
And foul in onward history,
And present sight, your ancient name.

THOMAS HARDY

THE MENIN ROAD, *Paul Nash.*

THE POETS

RUPERT CHAWNER BROOKE (1887–1915) once wrote that there were only three things in the world: to read poetry, to write poetry and best of all to live poetry. Educated at Rugby, where his father was a master, he had already published poems and was a fellow of King's College, Cambridge, when the Great War broke out. Initially ill-disposed towards the war, his mood changed and he patriotically enlisted, joining the Royal Naval Division. He saw service at Antwerp in 1914, but died of blood poisoning on the way to Gallipoli in April 1915.

GILBERT KEITH CHESTERTON (1874–1936), after an education at St Paul's, studied art at the Slade School before becoming a prolific and popular journalist. His most celebrated character, the detective Father Brown, first appeared in a series of short stories published in 1911, but after 1925 Chesterton published much of his work in his own journal, *G.K.'s Weekly*.

IVOR GURNEY (1890–1937) became a chorister at Gloucester cathedral and, as a pupil of the organist Sir Herbert Brewer, won a scholarship to the Royal College of Music. Serving in the ranks from 1916 till the end of the Great War, he was wounded, gassed and treated in military hospitals. His poems *Severn and Somme* were published in 1917, and his next volume, *War's Embers*, appeared in 1919. Though he took up his studies at the Royal College of Music, Gurney suffered such depression that he first was admitted to a mental hospital before transferring to the London Hospital, where he died of tuberculosis.

THOMAS HARDY (1840–1928), a stonemason's son, was born near Dorchester. He trained as a church architect before writing poetry. Between 1871 and 1896 he produced a succession of brilliant novels but, disillusioned by the poor critical reception of the last (*Jude the Obscure*), he thenceforth concentrated on poetry. A patriot during both the Boer War and World War I, he produced during both a body of subtle, fine verse.

THOMAS ERNEST HULME (1883–1916) was born in Staffordshire. From Newcastle-Under-

Lyme High School he went to St John's College, Cambridge, but was sent down in 1904. As well as mingling with philosophers, he founded a Poets' Club, inaugurating the Imagist school of poetry. In 1911 he attended the Philosophy Congress of Bologna and the following year the philosopher Henri Bergson arranged for him to be readmitted to Cambridge; but he soon left to write philosophy and translate Bergson's *Introduction to Metaphysics* and Georges Sorel's *Reflections on Violence*. Hulme's intellectual defence of militarism made it inevitable that he should enlist in 1914. He reached France the following year, was wounded and invalided home, went back to the front and, on 28 September 1917, was killed near Nieuport in Belgium.

GEOFFREY ANKETELL STUDDERT KENNEDY (1883–1929) was a Church of England clergyman who became a chaplain to the forces in 1916. He was soon the most famous serving padre – his racy language appealed to the men in the trenches, as did his hatred for the horrors of war, and his *Rough Rhymes of a Padre* added to his fame. His habit of handing out cigarettes to the troops earned him the nickname Woodbine Willie. After the war, decorated with the MC, he returned to his Worcestershire parish and, as a King's Chaplain, was subsequently appointed to the city living of St Edmund the King, where his inability to throw off the language of the

trenches, even when preaching, offended some. He died of influenza on a mission in Liverpool. As his body was brought through the streets, a working man pushed his way through the crowds to lay a packet of Woodbines on the coffin.

RUDYARD KIPLING (1865–1936) was born in Bombay and educated at the United Services College in Devon before becoming a journalist in Lahore. Fascinated by military life, he published his *Departmental Ditties* in 1886, after which he returned to England. For Queen Victoria's Diamond Jubilee he composed his celebrated *Recessional*; his children's stories became classics; he was offered, and declined, the office of poet laureate; thrice he declined the Order of Merit; and in 1907 he was awarded the Nobel prize for literature. When the Great War came, Kipling ceaselessly expressed his patriotism. In 1915 his only son, serving with the Irish Guards, was killed in action: Kipling sought solace by writing the history of his son's regiment and serving on the War Graves Commission.

DAVID HERBERT LAWRENCE (1885–1930), the fourth son of a miner, was born and educated in Nottingham before becoming a school teacher in Croydon. Shortly after the death of his mother in 1911, he published his first novel, and in the same year tuberculosis ended his teaching career. The following year he and Frieda Week-ley, the German wife of his former tutor in modern languages, eloped to Germany, but returned to Britain after their marriage. Lawrence deplored the Great War (though he twice volunteered for it). Renouncing industrialized civilization, he and Frieda travelled in Sicily, Ceylon, Australia and New Mexico, returning to Europe in 1925. His paintings were confiscated as obscene, and shortly before his death his last novel, *Lady Chatterley's Lover*, was banned.

FRANCIS LEDWIDGE (1887–1917), the eighth of nine children, was born in a labourer's cottage at Slane, Ireland. First apprenticed to a grocer at the age of fifteen, Francis successively became a farmhand, groom, roadworker and copper miner. He also began to write and his poems were published in the *Drogheda Independent* and the *Saturday Review*. When war broke out he enlisted in the Royal Inniskillin Fusiliers, seeing service at Gallipoli and Salonika, where he fell ill and was hospitalized. Recovered, he joined his unit in France. On 31 July 1917, as he was helping to mend a road near Ypres, a shell exploded. His chaplain wrote in his diary: 'Ledwidge killed, blown to bits; at Confession yesterday and Mass and Holy Communion this morning R.I.P.'

JOHN McCRAE (1872–1918) was a Canadian doctor and pathologist who was already writing poetry as a student at McGill University. 1914 saw him serving on the western front, but after the second battle of Ypres, he left to take charge of the medical department of No. 3 General Hospital, Boulogne. McCrae was recommended as consulting physician to the British Armies in France, but on 27 January 1918 he fell ill with pneumonia. He died the following day.

HUGH VIBART MacNAGHTEN (1862–1929), son of an Indian civil servant and grandson of a chairman of the East India Company, was born in Northern Ireland. Sent to Eton in 1874, he surpassed all his fellows in academic prowess both at school and, later, at Cambridge. Elected a fellow of Trinity, he returned to Eton in 1886, where he remained for the rest of his life. A skilled translator of Catullus and the Greek epigrams, he also published his own verse but, increasingly prey to depression, he drowned himself in the Thames on 11 August 1929.

ALICE CHRISTIANA GERTRUDE MEYNELL (1847–1922), though born in London, spent most of her childhood in Italy, where she began to write poetry. Converting to Roman Catholicism in 1872, she married the author Wilfred Meynell and bore him three children. Through him she was introduced to literary society. She achieved success with *The Rhythm of Life* (1893), *The Colour of Life* (1896) and *Hearts of Controversy* (1917), as well as with her verses.

WILFRED OWEN (1893–1918), born in Oswestry, was educated at the Birkenhead Institute and Shrewsbury Technical School. As a tutor in Bordeaux between 1913 and 1915, he came under the influence of contemporary innovative French poetry. Enlisting in October 1915, he took a commission in the Manchester Regiment the following June and sailed for France in December. From June 1917 he was in Craiglockhart hospital near Edinburgh, where he befriended Siegfried Sassoon. Returning to active service, he gained the MC, losing his life on 4 November 1918.

ISAAC ROSENBERG (1890–1918) was born into a Bristol Jewish family. Leaving school at the age of 14, he worked as an apprentice engraver, and attended evening art classes before going to the Slade School in 1911. The following year his first volume of poetry was published. After a brief stay in South Africa in 1914, he returned to Britain and enlisted – though unfit – in 1915. The following year he was in France, to be killed in action on 1 April 1918.

SIEGFRIED LORRAINE SASSOON (1886–1967) was born in Kent of Jewish parents, though he converted to Catholicism in 1957. Enlisting as a trooper in the Sussex Yeomanry and then commissioned into the Royal Welsh Fusiliers, Sassoon's bravery as an infantry officer in France won him the MC (under heavy fire he had brought back a wounded lance-corporal). He was also unsuccessfully recommended for a VC after capturing a German trench single-handed. But the horrors of war turned him into a pacifist, he attempted to have himself court-martialled for desertion and, on 30 July 1917, his protest against the continuation of the war was read out in the House of Commons. In 1918 Sassoon was posted to Palestine, before rejoining his former battalion in France. Wounded in the head on 13 July, he spent the rest of the war on permanent sick-leave.

ALAN SEEGER (1888–1916) was born in New York city and spent the first ten years of his life on Staten Island. Leaving Staten Island Academy, he went on to the Horace Mann School in Manhattan from where, in 1906, he entered Harvard, keeping aloof from most of his contemporaries, translating Dante and Ariosto and editing the *Harvard Monthly*. After graduation he spent two years in New York before moving to the Latin Quarter of Paris. Affecting to welcome the war as offering the possibility of fresh sensations, he enlisted in the French Foreign Legion, serving courageously on the Aisne and remaining with his regiment in Champagne during the offensive of September 1915. On 4 July 1916, he and his company went over the top near Belloy-en-Santerre. Seeger was last seen alive wounded, but still urging on his fellow soldiers. The following morning his body was found in a shell hole. He was awarded a posthumous Croix de Guerre and the Médaille Militaire.

CHARLES HAMILTON SORLEY (1895–1915), a Scot, spent his early life in Cambridge, where his father was a professor, and at Marlborough in Wiltshire, where he was educated. Just before the Great War broke out he spent six idyllic months in Germany. In spite of his liking for the Germans, Sorley immediately enlisted, reaching France in May 1915. He was killed at the battle of the Loos the following October.

PHILIP EDWARD THOMAS (1878–1917), a Londoner, was educated at St Paul's and at Lincoln College, Oxford. Writing for a living, he produced essays, topography and other ephemera, and turned to poetry only in 1914 under the influence of Robert Frost. Much of his verse was written on active service in France, where its roots in the Georgians and traditional English nature poetry, though never abandoned, became increasingly remote. Thomas was killed at Arras in April 1917.

KATHARINE TYNAN (1861–1931) was born into a Catholic farming family at Clondalkin, County Dublin, and educated at the Siena Convent, Drogehda. Married to a barrister and novelist, she lived in England, publishing her first book of poems, *Louise de la Vallière*, in 1885.

Befriending Yeats, Francis Ledwidge and Charles Stuart Parnell, she became a leading light in the Celtic literary revival, as well as earning her living by writing sentimental stories, including *The Way of a Maid*. Her early promise as a poet blossomed during the Great War, in which two of her sons served.

THEODORE PERCIVAL CAMERON WILSON (1889–1918) was a schoolmaster of Little Eaton, Derbyshire, who had written a couple of novels and published some poems in periodicals by the time he enlisted in the Grenadier Guards in August 1914. Transferring to the Sherwood Foresters as a second lieutenant, he had reached the rank of staff captain when he was killed in action in the Somme valley on 23 March 1918.

WILLIAM BUTLER YEATS (1865–1939), of Irish ancestry, spent much of his childhood with his grandparents in Sligo. When his family returned to a home near Dublin, Yeats's education continued at the Dublin High School, where he was soon producing precocious poetry. Under the influence of AE (George William Russell) and of Madame Blavatsky, Yeats embraced mystical theosophy. Established in London he was encouraged by William Morris, Arthur Symons and W.E. Henley, while his Irish connections led him to support Gaelic literary nationalism. He was awarded the Nobel prize for literature in 1923.

INDEX of FIRST LINES

ᴀCKNOWLEDGEMENTS

The editor is much indebted to Andrew Best for his ready help in finding illustrations for this book, and to Monica Harding, who first alerted him to the poetry of Francis Ledwidge and sought out the poet's biographical details. Mrs Melva Croll of Manchester City Art Galleries has been exceptionally helpful. In addition, the editor would like to thank Mrs Corinne Cherrad and Dr Bernadette Nelson of the Ashmolean Museum, Oxford, and Neil Bingham of the R.I.B.A. collections, Portman Square, London.

The publisher would like to thank the following museums and galleries for supplying illustrations:
ASHMOLEAN MUSEUM, OXFORD: p.14 Gloucestershire Landscape, *John Nash*.
HUDDERSFIELD ART GALLERY, KIRKLEES METROPOLITAN COUNCIL: p.25 Tea in the Bed-Sitter, *Harold Gilman*.
IMPERIAL WAR MUSEUM, LONDON: front jacket Heavy Artillery, *Colin U. Gill*; p.2 A Shell Dump, France, *William P. Roberts*; p.12 The Underworld: Taking Cover in a Tube Station During a London Air Raid, *Walter Bayes*; p.17 The Balloon Apron, *Frank Dobson*; p.19 Ruined Country, *Paul Nash*; p.20 Oppy Wood, *John Nash*; p.22 Ready to Start (Self-Portrait), *William Orpen*; p.26 A Torpedoed Tramp Steamer off the Longships, Cornwall, *Geoffrey S. Allfree*; p.28 The Die-Hards, *Eric H. Kennington*; p.36 Observation of Fire, *Colin U. Gill*; p.38 An Impression of Lens, France, seen from an Aeroplane, *Richard C. Carline*; p.40 The Kensingtons at Laventie, *Eric H. Kennington*; p.43 British Scouts Leaving Their Aerodrome on Patrol, over the Asiago Plateau, Italy, *Sydney W. Carline*; p.48 In Billets, Winter: Rations Up, *Herbert A. Budd*; p.51 On the Departure Platform, *Bernard Meninsky*; p.52 The Somme Battlefield, *Miss Oliver*; p.55 Evening, after a Push, *Colin U. Gill*; p.57 The Bombardment of Gorizia, 21 August 1917, *Elliott Seabrooke*; p.58 We Are Making a New World, *Paul Nash*; p.60 The Landscape, Hill 60, *Paul Nash*; p.63 Over the Top, *John Nash*; p.64 Troops Resting (detail), *C.R.W. Nevinson*; p.69 Operating on a Slightly Wounded Man in a Regimental Aid Post, *Austin O. Spare*; p.70 Bombing: Night, *William Orpen*; p.73 A Group of Soldiers, *C.R.W. Nevinson*; p.75 Sunset: Ruin of the Hospice, Wytschaete, *Paul Nash*; p.76 Wounded Men on Duppas Hill, Croydon, *Dorothy J. Coke*; p.79 The Battle of 'The Pips', 24 April 1917, *William T. Wood*; p.82 The Women's Land Army and German Prisoners, *Randolphe Schwabe*; p.85 The Advance, *W. Bernard Adeney*; p.86 Interrogation, *Francis Dodd*; p.88 A Battery Shelled, *Percy Wyndham Lewis*; p.90 Dead Germans in a Trench, *William Orpen*; p.93 L'Enfer, *Georges Leroux*; p.94 Poilu and Tommy, *William Orpen*; p.97 The Sisters, *Edmund Dulac*; p.98 Spring in the Trenches, Ridge Wood, 1917, *Paul Nash*; p.101 Irish Troops in the Judean Hills Surprised by a Turkish Bombardment, *Henry Lamb*; p.103 The Captive, *Colin U. Gill*; p.104 Artillery Drivers in the Snow, *A. Neville Lewis*; p.107 Travoys Arriving with Wounded at a Dressing Station at Smol, Macedonia, September 1916, *Stanley Spencer*; p.110 Gassed (detail), *John Singer Sargent*; p.113 The Menin Road, *Paul Nash*.
MANCHESTER CITY ART GALLERIES: p.81 Advanced Dressing Station on the Struma, *Henry Lamb*.
NATIONAL GALLERY OF CANADA, OTTAWA: p.33 Sappers at Work: A Canadian Tunnelling Company, *David Bomberg*; p.47 Dazzle-Ships in Drydock at Liverpool, *Edward Wadsworth*.
NATIONAL MUSEUM OF WALES, CARDIFF: p.31 Girl in Blue, *Gwen John*.
THE TATE GALLERY, LONDON: p.35 Farm at Watendlath, *Dora Carrington*; p.44 La Mitrailleuse, *C.R.W. Nevinson*; p.109 Merry-Go-Round, *Mark Gertler*.

The publisher is also grateful to Mr George Sassoon for granting permission to include the following works by Siegfried Sassoon: p.72 'The General'; p.84 'Blighters'; p.91 'Reconciliation'; p.96 'Glory of Women'.